THE FUNNIEST ARSENAL QUOTES... EVER! 2

Also available

I Didn't See It: The funniest Arsene Wenger quotes... ever!

The Funniest Arsenal Quotes... Ever!

The Funniest Liverpool Quotes... Ever!

The Funniest Chelsea Quotes... Ever!

The Funniest West Ham Quotes... Ever!

The Funniest Spurs Quotes... Ever!

The Funniest Man City Quotes... Ever!

The Funniest Newcastle Quotes... Ever!

The Funniest United Quotes... Ever!

The Funniest Leeds Quotes... Ever!

The Funniest Boro Quotes... Ever!

The Funniest Forest Quotes... Ever!

The Funniest Sunderland Quotes... Ever!

The Funniest Leicester Quotes... Ever!

The Funniest Saints Quotes... Ever!

The Funniest Everton Quotes... Ever!

The Funniest Villa Quotes... Ever!

The Funniest QPR Quotes... Ever!

The Funniest England Quotes... Ever!

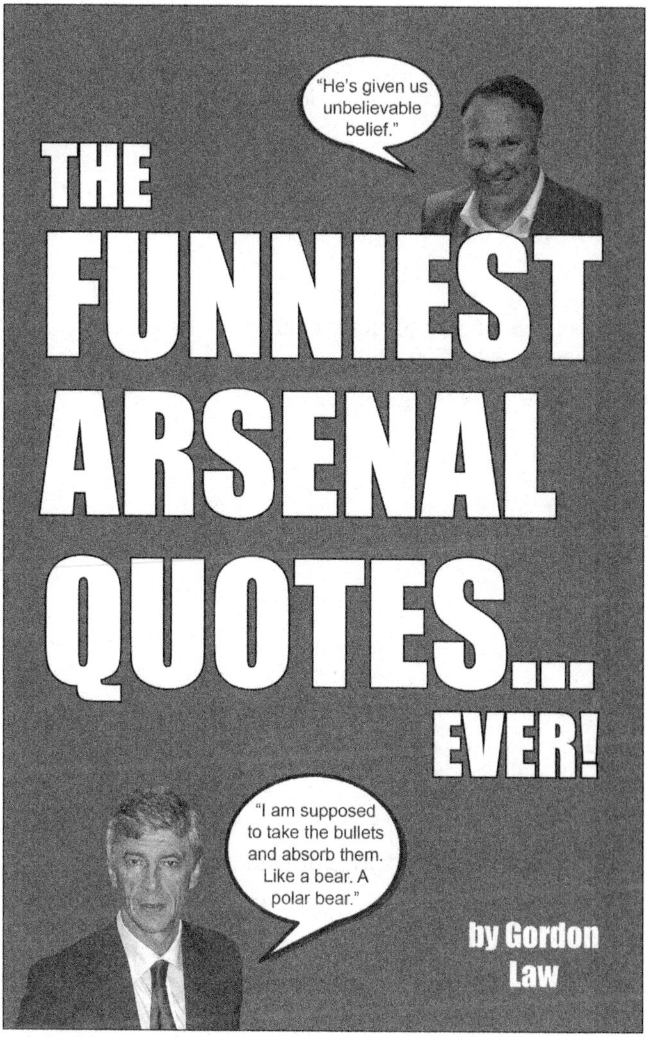
"He's given us unbelievable belief."
THE FUNNIEST ARSENAL QUOTES... EVER!
"I am supposed to take the bullets and absorb them. Like a bear. A polar bear."
by Gordon Law

Printed in Europe and the USA

ISBN: 9798755728430
Imprint: Independently published

Photos courtesy of: katatonia82/Shutterstock.com; Cosmin Iftode/Shutterstock.com; Mitch Gunn/Shutterstock.com.

Contents

THE FUNNIEST ARSENAL QUOTES... EVER! 2

FIELD OF DREAMS

"My behaviour was not acceptable... I rang my wife after the game, and she's usually very supportive, but she said, 'I think you've gone and done it now'. It was the first time she'd ever said anything like that."

Martin Keown on goading Ruud van Nistelrooy after he missed a last-minute penalty for Man United

"What is to regret after that? I wanted to go from A to B and somebody confronted me without any sign of welcome."

Arsene Wenger plays down a dugout argy-bargy with Jose Mourinho

"Like everyone says, I always score in small games. I think today must have been a small game again."

Thierry Henry's barb at Jose Mourinho after scoring against Chelsea

"I cannot sit there and be placid like I am on dope."

Arsene Wenger on his touchline antics

"Referees seem to be treating star players as a kind of trophy. They go home to their wives and say, 'Guess what – I sent off that Emmanuel Petit today'."

Emmanuel Petit

"Last year we won the game against Everton with a 25 per cent chance of winning, you win 3-2. Last weekend, it was a 67 per cent chance of winning, any Premier League game in history, and a nine per cent chance of losing, and you lose. Three per cent against Burnley and you lose, seven per cent against Spurs, and you lose."

Mikel Arteta confuses us

"I haven't seen that. I don't know anything about it. I don't know what you're talking about."

Arsene Wenger somehow didn't see the on-field spat between teammates Emmanuel Adebayor and Nicklas Bendtner

"I want to apologise to the managers because I actually dived."

Honest Theo Walcott admits to trying to win a penalty against Leeds

"It's just a joke. He's been bad all evening. He's been a joke all evening, whistling against us. I don't know why he's here tonight. I think it's a joke."

Robin van Persie believes referee Massimo Busacca was a joke

"Once again, I had to manage to score all on my own."

The sulky Nicolas Anelka

"I can shake hands with who I want."

Arsene Wenger defends not handshaking with Mark Hughes after defeat to Man City

"At one point he questioned why I was over on his side of the technical area. He may have been a little bit aggrieved by that, but I would suggest he was more aggrieved that his team got beat."

Hughes suggests Wenger is a bad loser

"I don't deny that I'm a bad loser but I would have done exactly the same if we had won or lost."

Wenger continues

"Against Stoke I mark my 500th game and I believe I have shaken hands 497 times."

Wenger backs up his reasoning

"I don't know who it is. I am going to answer it. John Spencer. Can I answer? OK, good morning. Hi, I am Unai Emery. How are you? We are working."

Unai Emery answers a journalist's phone during a press conference

"I'm not upset. I'm upset because we lost the game."

Arsene Wenger after defeat to Sevilla. So which is it?

"It was like someone was holding them with a PS3 controller, controlling them all the time."

Theo Walcott on Barcelona's display against the Gunners

"If somebody stamps on your head in that way, you wouldn't say, 'Thank you very much' and turn the other cheek. Only Jesus Christ did that."

Arsene Wenger backs Robin van Persie

"I just told him there, I still owe him dinner."

Arsene Wenger on his touchline row with Kenny Dalglish

"A goalkeeper should never be beaten from that distance."

David Seaman on Ronaldinho's World Cup goal from 47 yards – before he conceded a 43-yarder from Chelsea's Gianfranco Zola

"It didn't disturb me too much and I don't expect to be banned. Do you want me sent to jail?"

Arsene Wenger after being sent off during Arsenal's 2-2 draw with Portsmouth

"It was like a car crash."

Mikel Arteta on how Arsenal felt conceding four within 20 minutes against Liverpool

"I'm not superstitious or anything like that, but I'll just hope we'll play our best and put it in the lap of the gods."

Terry Neill

"I forgot it, didn't I! I'm not used to it. My last hat-trick was probably for United's reserves."

Danny Welbeck fails to collect his match ball after a treble against Galatasaray

"Leave me alone for... sake!"

An angry Arsene Wenger manages to avoid saying the 'f word' to reporters in the post-match press conference

"That was f*cking embarrassing! Apologies to anyone who sat through 90mins of that game."
Wojciech Szczesny following Arsenal's 5-0 defeat to Liverpool

"I cannot believe that you, as journalists, question a player's contract. No one points a gun to your head when you sign a contract. I respect my contract, but every week I get asked questions about players who are under contract."
Arsene Wenger on Cesc Fabregas' deal

"Good ebening!"
Unai Emery

TALKING BALLS

"Marc plays only for himself. He makes me run like a dog."

Nicolas Anelka on Marc Overmars

"I do not know why a player at 25 wants to tell me all about their big experiences. When I consider the age I am now, I would have a lot to tell people. But it seems to be an English habit to come out with books that nobody needs."

Jens Lehmann on Ashley Cole's book

"I'll be really pleased to see Tottenham in the Europa League next season."

Wojciech Szczesny has a dig at the rivals

"Thierry Henry came to Arsenal and he left.
Cesc Fabregas came to Arsenal and he left.
Why not Adebayor? I am not obliged to die at
Arsenal."

Emmanuel Adebayor is happy to leave

"I was very young the first time he was at the
club but he is still a nutcase!"

Wojciech Szczesny on Jens Lehmann

"We play a bit of FIFA together and that was
just a simple 'X'."

**Theo Walcott on why Arsenal are such a
good passing side**

"I'm not one for singing around the campfire, that is more Nicklas Bendtner's style."

Andrey Arshavin

"I'm very excited to see him in the flesh and play with him."

Theo Walcott on Mesut Ozil

"He's a Duracell battery. He never stops."

Olivier Giroud on Alexis Sanchez

"He is a good, good, good, great goalscorer."

Mathieu Flamini on Thierry Henry

"I got into trouble with teachers at school for too much chat. I've always been this way, I was born this way."

Wojciech Szczesny on his vocal presence

"He wasn't high on anyone's Christmas card list."

David O'Leary says goalie Jimmy Rimmer wasn't liked by everyone

"I'm a very good goalkeeper... he knows."

Robin van Persie backs himself after Jens Lehmann was almost sent off at Blackpool

OFF THE PITCH

"Now I am watching an English series to improve my English. Peaky Blinders. It is good but it is difficult (to understand), from Birmingham. And it's very aggressive. But it's good, it's good."

Unai Emery says Peaky Blinders is helping him learn English

"If I had it in my power to introduce a ban on women driving cars and to withdraw all their licences, I would do it without thinking twice. In my opinion a woman and a man are two absolutely different creatures."

Andrey Arshavin

"When Patrick Vieira came over from AC Milan, he didn't know a word of English. We gave him accommodation, phone, car and an English teacher. I talked to Patrick in fluent French and before a game I asked in French, can you speak a bit of English to me? Patrick nodded and replied, 'Tottenham are sh*t'."

David Dein

"My parents live with me and are always by my side. My sisters stayed in Brazil. With food and stuff, I have no problem because my mother cooks at home and it is easier for me."

Gabriel Martinelli the mummy's boy

"I've been fascinated by leather for a very long time and discovering the creations of Jean-Claude Jitrois was for me some kind of a revelation."

Emmanuel Petit

"Dear Ken, welcome back to football. Let hostilities commence. Let's have lunch."

David Dein in a fax to new Leeds chairman Ken Bates

"If I have sex on the night before a game, I lose all feeling in my feet."

Freddie Ljungberg

"I've prohibited her from complaining about life in England. Since then there have been no more criticisms."

Andrey Arshavin silences his partner

"When we go out in the evening I like to go for it. I love the traditional English gentleman look with cuff-links, highly-polished shoes and even a money clip."

David Seaman

"I've lived here for seven years and watched it twice. It's even worse than French TV."

Gael Clichy on EastEnders

"If I go into a bar and have a lager shandy, word goes back that I'm knocking back bottles of champagne. By the time it gets to the papers or my manager at Arsenal, it's me lying in the gutter."

Charlie Nicholas

Q: "What's your first impression of Malaysia?"
Robin van Persie: "We've seen a very nice airport."

"He took the product of his wife, and never trust your wife."

Arsene Wenger says Yaya Toure's failed drugs test was a result of taking a diet pill

Q: "If you could be a woman for a day, who would you be?"

Jack Wilshere: "I'd probably be Cheryl Cole. Just to see what attention she gets and that."

"Parking is a disaster for me. I usually have to park a mile away from the place I need."

Andrey Arshavin

"Those who have been out on the town and smell of booze the next morning are the ones I set out after. I chase them during training and won't leave them alone. I'm a pest from the first minute to the last. "

Dennis Bergkamp

"Ever since I have been a professional footballer it has been harder for me to go out and not be noticed. Especially by female fans. I have never had any problems with women; I often get letters from girls, who send me their phone numbers and photos."

Samir Nasri

Q: "Hi, Andrey! My question will seem stupid, but I want to know. Why do players play football in boots rather than in other footwear? You're so handsome! You're the best! You are super!"

Andrey Arshavin: "It's better than playing in fins or on skates."

"She should keep herself quiet and not complain."
Peter Hill-Wood responds to claims from Lady Nina Bracewell-Smith that the Arsenal board is a chauvinistic old boys' club

"This is so funny, but my brothers are older than me – I was the youngest, and they used to tease me about a kids' TV character called ALF. Do you know him? ALF the Alien, my God he was so ugly and I was so scared of him. My brothers used to say, 'Be careful, ALF is going to get you tonight!' They went too far with it!"
Olivier Giroud's childhood fear of 80s TV character ALF

"I was born in the north of Spain, with the rain. Then I lived a lot in Spain, with the sun. I love the sun a lot. But also, we need the rain. Maybe if it was raining less, it'd be better."

Unai Emery on living in England

"Just don't bring your ugly face to the Emirates."

Emmanuel Frimpong gets annoyed with Piers Morgan's criticism of the team

"When I was a kid, we had two kittens. I cannot now remember their gender. And we also had a hamster. However, they all disappeared under unclear circumstances."

Andrey Arshavin

"We have made an undertaking to Arsene Wenger and his family not to name our new coach."

Peter Hill-Wood lets the cat out of the bag at the 1996 AGM

"What does 'British food' mean? I heard about fish and chips but I do not eat it. I heard about ales! Ales! A special drink like beer but without gas! I've not tried it."

Andrey Arshavin

"The thing I miss most about London is bread and butter."

Thierry Henry after leaving for Barcelona

"I know [Vieira] was a very good player. But I wouldn't know the details."

Benjamin White's surprise admission he has never seen club legend Patrick Vieira play

"The biggest issue was that I was so high most of the time, I didn't have a clue who or what I was gambling on. £10,000 on the Eurovision song contest, £5,000 on a bowls match on BBC Two, £20,000 on an NFL game."

Paul Merson

"I would like to be Eddie Murphy, the comedian."

Emmanuel Eboue

"At home I eat soups and Russian salads...
There are lots of cut tomatoes, cut cucumbers
and a few leaves. But here? Opposite way!
There are a lot of leaves and one cut tomato
and two slices of cucumber!"

Andrey Arshavin

"I've learned [English] from watching cartoons.
Now I've progressed to films."

Gilles Grimandi

"My secret is adapting to the country I am in.
Here I eat roast beef and Yorkshire pudding."

Arsene Wenger

Unai Emery: "I think the best thing for the next match is for Matteo to cut his hair. And this problem is finished, like [with] Fellaini."

Reporter: "Have you told him that?"

Emery: "No, I respect a lot the players' hair, their colour."

The manager jokes that Matteo Guendouzi should style his hair like Marouane Fellaini

"When I come to the training ground I always try to make everyone happy at Arsenal. I am happy if you are happy. That's why I have said that after my career I will become an actor."

Emmanuel Eboue

"I'm like 90 per cent of footballers. When we meet a woman, we're thinking, 'Are they just after me for the money?'."

Sol Campbell

"I'd like to be a dog. Dogs are nice. They can sleep any time, they wag their tails and on top of that they can get stroked all the time."

Emmanuel Petit

"I wasn't nervous. He just said he prefers me as a footballer not a writer."

Theo Walcott gets approval from England boss Fabio Capello on his book

WENGER'S WISDOM

"Eduardo [da Silva] is like the guy who stands on the motorway and gets run down by the lorry coming up the wrong side."

Arsene Wenger

"You should be happy; he [Rob Holding] is English, he is 20 years old, but I'm sorry he didn't cost £55m, so it cannot be good."

Wenger gets sarcastic with reporters

"With normal mathematics, minus 80 is minus 80. It's not on the surface, it is 80 miles below water – and to survive so deep is normally very difficult."

The manager on Chelsea's £80m losses

"The only way he will fly to Athens is if he turns into a pigeon."

Wenger on Dennis Bergkamp's chances of playing against Panathinaikos

"I realised when I joined Arsenal that the back four were all university graduates in the art of defending and Tony Adams was the Doctor of defence."

Wenger gets scholarly

"If you want to win the title, one thing you need is consistent consistency."

Wenger after losing to Sunderland

"With a team you live in a tunnel and sometimes you have to go down and flirt with hell to see how much you can deal with that, so that you become stronger. But you go quickly to hell and very slowly to heaven."

Wenger puzzles us with this one

"Maybe I will play with six strikers as we have to score goals."

The manager's radical solution to overturn a 4-0 deficit against AC Milan

"Sport is full of legends who are in fact cheats."

Wenger gets cynical

"It just shows how effective our training is! He trained here once and is bought by PSG!"

Wenger claims credit for David Beckham's move to Paris Saint-Germain

"They are not used to him being complimentary about a referee. This was a shock for the FA!"

Wenger on news that Sir Alex Ferguson has been charged for praising Howard Webb prior to United's game with Chelsea

"I would not like to be too mathematical, but they say on average it is 10.2 points which qualify you."

The boss does indeed get mathematical

"He was one years old when I came to Arsenal."

The long-serving boss on Serge Gnabry

"I personally don't know who will win the league and I have managed 1,600 games. So if Nani knows, he must be 1,600 times more intelligent than I am."

He hits back at Nani who claimed Arsenal have no chance of winning the title

"We can all understand that we can make wrong decisions, but after that it becomes dictatorship."

Wenger blasts UEFA after his charge of improper conduct

"You've certainly tried to go out with a girl but find she has chosen someone else. You don't commit suicide."

Wenger is not worried if Luis Suarez signs for Real Madrid

"We are not after any French player, you can forget that... they go to Newcastle."

The manager has a laugh at the Magpies

"Spurs have had all these great players. They had Ginola before. They had... Anderton."

The Gunners boss takes a swipe at their North London rivals

"For example, if you lose your hair and you've taken something to make your hair grow, it might not be good for the rest of your body."
The Frenchman's hair-raising analogy

"Look at the state I am in, I took up coaching very young!"
He advises Thierry Henry not to get into coaching too early

"Maybe I will go to church over the weekend!"
Wenger looks for some divine intervention before the Champions League draw

"We are short [up front] because Theo [Walcott] is not very tall!"

The manager on Arsenal's injury woes

"I have selection solutions, not selection problems."

Wenger's interesting take on his squad

Martin Tyler: "Am I too romantic to think players should stay on their feet and not make it a problem for referees?"

Arsene Wenger: "I don't say you are too romantic but you are romantic."

He flirts with the Sky Sports commentator

"It's just inflammation – too much French salami."

On why Laurent Koscielny won't need surgery on his achilles injury

"They have my credit card number, and we will say, 'How much do you need this week? Let's do it'."

Wenger on meeting with the FA's disciplinary panel again

"Apparently I am to blame because I don't produce enough English players!"

Wenger on taking the flak for England's defeat against Croatia

"I'm not interested. What can a job like that do for me? You would have to be a masochist."
The Arsenal manager on taking charge of the England team

"If we have not got a game for a while, and we have lost, there are times when I have not gone out for days. It really hurts. People who live around you suffer with you, so the only thing I can do is try to get out of other people's way. I try to be like a dog who is sick – I go away into quarantine and come back when I'm cured!"
It's a dog's life for the Frenchman

"I am the French bin Laden."

After refusing to send half his Arsenal team to Australia for a friendly with France

"His feet look the same as ten-past-ten on a clock."

Wenger on Robert Pires

"I haven't seen it, but it looks generous."

Wenger's classic response to reporters

"My biggest regret since coming to England is not winning the Worthington Cup."

Is Wenger joking?

"I have to sit down with him and see where we stand."

The boss has a see-saw relationship with Patrick Vieira

"Imagine the worst – we lose Fabregas and Nasri. You can't then pretend you are a big club. A big club holds on to big players."

Wenger – before losing Fabregas and Nasri

"I used to promise my wife I would retire at 55. Then I got to 55 and said, 'Make that 60'. Now I don't speak about it any more."

Wenger wants to stay out of the house

GAME FOR A LAUGH

"People who were perhaps five at the time I went to Arsenal, or were not even born, feel strongly about it. Who is perpetuating this? It is incredible."

Sol Campbell on the abuse he still gets from making the switch from Spurs to Arsenal

"English football is hard work – you have to run all the time."

Nwankwo Kanu

"I want to be remembered as a small Russian guy who did some magical things that people did not understand how he did."

Andrey Arshavin

"The award means a lot – and at the same time nothing. It is something I hadn't given a moment's thought to."

Nicolas Anelka on failing to collect his PFA Young Player of the Year award

"I have always told my family that if Ghana call me, I will personally ride my own bicycle from England to Ghana."

Emmanuel Frimpong says he will reject England

"If I played flawlessly in all the matches I would be Lionel Messi."

Thomas Vermaelen

"I have the impression that I'm playing matches against ghosts. I don't really know whether they are dreams or nightmares."

Nicolas Anelka

"The ball is in my court and the show must go on."

Olivier Giroud loves a cliche

"Chelsea players are always bitching against the referees. I really cannot understand that. Just shut the f*ck up and focus on playing football. If you want to witness a lot of complaints, you should just go the bakery or something."

Robin van Persie

"I went home afterwards and just cried. I was very upset, very sad and I was ashamed."

An emotional Denilson after Arsenal's Carling Cup final defeat

Sky Sports' Gary Cotterill: "Is it Ben or Benjamin?"

Benjamin White: "It's actually Benjamin."

Cotterill: "Why?"

White: "It's my name."

Insightful questioning from the interviewer

"I am a Nigerian and I will remain a Nigerian until the day I die."

Kanu

"I must say I personally prefer the FC Cologne anthem over the Liverpool one."

Lukas Podolski did not think much of the singing at Anfield

"I am German when we win but I am an immigrant when we lose."

Mesut Ozil on retiring from international football

"Would like to congratulate Mario Balotelli... even if he doesn't know who I am."

Jack Wilshere after coming second in the Golden Boy awards

"We sometimes have to put the bullfighter's uniform in the cupboard."

Samir Nasri

"He is a coach sent by God."

Alexander Hleb pays a big tribute to Arsene Wenger

"Very good win gays!"

Andre Santos wins the award for best Freudian Tweet of the Year

"Arsene Wenger is like our dad."

Emmanuel Eboue

"At the moment I'm just swallowing it all as part of the humiliation but I think – and this is aimed at my dear manager – one shouldn't humiliate players for too long."

Jens Lehmann is not happy with his boss

"How you have to play football in England... Going for a high ball I use my elbow or I'm dead."

Thierry Henry

"My goals in Holland were known as 'stiffies', which means something quite different in England of course."

Dennis Bergkamp

"I am not a clown who will just sit out his contract on the stands."

Lukas Podolski takes aim at Arsene Wenger

"I felt a bit like Lady Gaga."

Theo Walcott is happy with his reception on the club's Asian tour

"I've learned never to say never. Then again, I think I can safely say I wouldn't join Tottenham!"

Patrick Vieira

Q: "Would you rather sign for Spurs or retire?"

Mesut Ozil: "Easy question. Retire!"

PUNDIT PARADISE

"If it doesn't go right tonight, Wenger has got another leg up his sleeve."

Glenn Hoddle on the two-legged League Cup semi-final

"Pink is a woman's colour, or so my missus tells me."

Ron 'Chopper' Harris on Nicklas Bendtner's pink boots

"Had [Martin] Taylor not broken Eduardo's leg with that tackle we'd have said, 'That's a leg-breaking tackle'."

Matt Le Tissier

"Throwing food is what children do. We were real men. We'd have chinned them."

George Best after Arsenal players threw pizza at Sir Alex Ferguson

"Arsene Wenger built a stadium at Arsenal, though he didn't actually build a stadium."

Tony Gale

"I think Arsene Wenger should have been fined several times over for his team's behaviour – 40 sendings-off in his first five years as manager is nothing short of a disgrace."

Brian Clough

"We've just seen the teams and they both look like they've come here to play football."

Frank Clark

"Fabregas literally carries 10 yards of space around in his shorts."

Ray Wilkins

"They've scored 32 goals in every game this season."

Alan Parry

"Martin Keown is up everyone's backside."

Trevor Brooking

"If Wenger is still here in 10 years and Arsenal haven't won any trophies, will he still be here?"
Steve Claridge

"Arsenal's touch and movement are amazing. I hope the listeners are watching this."
Chris Waddle on Radio 5 Live

"The goal that Charlton scored has aroused Arsenal."
George Graham

"Arsenal have literally been passed to death."
Jamie Redknapp

"Arsenal are doing just enough, which isn't enough."

Martin Keown

"How important will the goalkeeper be for Arsenal tonight?"

Ian Payne just before a penalty shoot-out against Roma

"The 1-0 to the Arsenal era that brought them such success has moved on to a very different kind of era, a 2-0 in the Champions League and a 6-1 and a 4-1 in the Premier League."

A bit of a mouthful for George Hamilton

"It's Arsenal 0, Everton 1. And the longer it stays like that the more you've got to fancy Everton to win."

John Motson

"It's a great satisfaction to see two teams I coached draw 0-0."

George Graham on a goalless Arsenal v Tottenham clash

"Arsenal and Spurs? No chance. The best two clubs in London are still Stringfellows and the Hippodrome."

Terry McDermott

"The Arsenal defence is skating close to the wind."

Jack Charlton

"Arsene Wenger uses the FA Cup to bleed his youngsters."

Alvin Martin

"What a goal by Bergkamp! One for the puritans."

Capital Gold commentator

"And Seaman, just like a falling oak, manages to change direction."

John Motson

"Arsenal are quick to credit Bergkamp with laying on 75 per cent of their nine goals."

Tony Gubba

"Van Persie is the right player for Arsenal – he can open a can of worms."

Paul Merson

"Arsenal have been written off so often you can't write them off."

Matt Le Tissier

"The Arsenal youth team is full of young players."

Robbie Earle

"After that goal you could literally see Arsenal's players deflating."

Mick Quinn

"Arsenal could have got away with a 0-0 if it wasn't for the two goals."

Des Lynam

"Arsenal owe a great deal of debtitude to the keeper."

Matt Le Tissier

"For Arsenal, the sight is in end."

David Pleat

"I've no idea what Arsenal paid for him. It was four million plus."

Charlie Nicholas

"Only Arsenal have scored more goals than Arsenal this season."

Dickie Davies

"If Arsenal lose now, I'll eat my heart."

Craig Burley

"Nicolas Anelka left Arsenal for £23million and they built a training ground on him."

Kevin Keegan

"Arsene would've thought in the past, 'Thierry will get me 20, Pires 15, Ljungberg 12'. That's 50 goals."

George Graham

"They've really eked this one out. Like coal miners mining their seam until they finally reach the surface with their precious black gold."

George Hamilton as Arsenal leave it late

"Arsenal literally finished the game after 15 minutes."

Ian Wright

"It's amazing what the sight of four gentlemen with red crosses on their backs can do to injured players."

Jon Champion on Freddie Ljungberg's miraculous recovery

"Why should I? [watch the Charity Shield]. I'm no longer part of Arsenal and it doesn't interest me. To hell with the English people."

Nicolas Anelka

"If you gave Arsene Wenger 11 players and told him to pick his team, this would be it."

TalkSport's Andy Gray

"I think Charlie George was one of Arsenal's all-time great players. A lot of people might not agree with that, but I personally do."

Jimmy Greaves

"What's it like being in Bethlehem, the place where Christmas began? I suppose it's like seeing Ian Wright at Arsenal."

Simon Fanshawe, TalkRadio

"They played Arsenal and got their backsides felt."

Craig Burley

"And Arsenal now have plenty of time to dictate the last few seconds."

Peter Jones

"An unstoppable shot… that should've been saved?"

Michael Owen on Tomas Rosicky's rocket strike for the Gunners against Spurs

"He's multi-lingual. He'll say 'ouch' in five different languages."

Mark Lawrenson on cunning linguist Philippe Senderos

"Arsenal's defence will be a worry going forward."

Kenny Cunningham

"That's Arsenal – they're either brilliant or inconsistent."

Jamie Redknapp

"Arsenal need crispier passing."

Sam Matterface

"If Arsenal don't finish third, they might not finish in third place."

Alvin Martin

"Arsenal are in tough competition for fourth with the likes of Spurs, Everton and Arsenal."
Paul Merson

"John Cross is feeling very boyish about Arsenal's chances."
Alan Brazil

"Three minutes to go – this is where Arsenal normally get a last-minute goal."
Sir Alan Sugar

"The game is balanced in Arsenal's favour."
John Motson

"It wasn't only the manner Arsenal got beat, it was the way they got beat."

Warren Barton

"Terrific one-stuff football from Arsenal there."

Marcus Buckland

"Arsene took too long to replace those players, and they were irreplaceable."

Ray Wilkins

"Arsene Wenger did a brilliant job, but the cupboard has been dry for seven years."

Mick Quinn

"Aaron Ramsey hasn't always been the flavour of the Arsenal fans' eyes."

Craig Burley

"Arsene Wenger has bought some tall defenders. There was Edu, then came Sol Campbell, Kolo Toure and even Ralph Lauren was over six foot."

Perry Groves

John Champion: "An interesting fact is that of Arsenal's last 56 goals, Thierry Henry has only scored 12 of them."

Ron Atkinson: "Yeah, but he created the other 40."

"Arsenal are coming forward in wave after wave of waves."

Alvin Martin

"There's no finer sight in football than when Thierry Henry opens his legs and just comes on the ball."

Terry Paine

"Everyone's got tough games coming up. Manchester United have got Arsenal, Arsenal have got Manchester United and Leeds have got Leeds."

Kevin Keegan

"As positive as Arsenal were, I thought they were quite negative."

Peter Reid

"I'm a great lover of Jack Wilshere's."

Ray Wilkins

"When Walcott's in that position he always sometimes doesn't deliver."

Alan Shearer

"Fabregas misses out but Samir Nasri will be the benefactor."

Jamie Redknapp

"The match has become quite unpredictable, but it still looks as though Arsenal will win the cup."

John Motson

"Not many teams will come to Arsenal and get anything, home or away."

Kevin Keegan

"I watched Arsenal playing some of the best football I've ever seen and yet they couldn't have scored in a brothel with two grand in their pockets."

Ian Holloway

"You can't really grumble at the red card but it's very harsh."

Michael Owen after Gabriel was sent off

"And the average age of the Arsenal defence is over 100 years."

Hong Kong TV commentator

"It's always very satisfying to beat Arsenal, as indeed Arsenal would admit."

Peter Jones

"I want to see Arsenal really push off this season."

Alvin Martin

FAN
FEVER

"You're just a fat Eddie Murphy!"

Arsenal fans to Jimmy Floyd Hasselbaink

"Tango, Tango, what's the score?"

Supporters to Hull boss Phil Brown at The Emirates

"Donkey won the derby!"

Gunners fans hail Tony Adams after his winner against Tottenham

"One Lily Savage, there's only one Lily Savage."

Directed at Blackburn's Robbie Savage

"He's tall, he's quick, his name's a porno flick.
Emmanuel, Emmanuel."

A ditty for Emmanuel Petit

"Peter Shilton, Peter Shilton, does your missus
know you're here?"

**Arsenal fans wind up the goalkeeper after a
reported affair**

"We'll race you back to London, yes we will."

**Arsenal supporters mock the home fans at
Old Trafford (to the tune of She'll be Coming
Round The Mountain)**

"Oh, Teddy, Teddy. You went to Man United and you won f*ck all."

Arsenal fans rib former Tottenham striker Teddy Sheringham after the Gunners win the double in 1998

"Oh, Teddy, Teddy. You might have won the treble but you're still a c*nt!"

The Gooners update their song

"Osama, woooah. Osama, woooah. He follows Arsenal. He's hiding in Kabul."

Chant for Osama bin Laden, a reported Gunners fan

"You're not fit to referee!"

Chant aimed at ref Mark Clattenburg who was being treated for an injury

"Alex Hleb, woooah. Alex Hleb, woooah. He came from Belarus. To sell cheap fags and booze."

A tribute to the midfielder

"Let's talk about Cesc baby. Let's talk about Flamini. Let's talk about Theo Walcott, Freddie Ljungberg and Henry. Let's talk about Cesc!"

A catchy song to the tune of Let's Talk About Sex

"Big f*cking German. We've got a big f*cking German. Big f*cking German. We've got a big f*cking German..."

A tribute to Per Mertesacker

"Christmas time, valium and wine. Children indulging in serious crime. With mum on the heroine and dad snorting coke. Christmas is magic when you support Stoke..."

Sang to the tune of Mistletoe And Wine

"World Cup and you f*cked it up!"

Taunting referee Graham Poll after he wrongly issued three yellows at the finals

"One Song. We've only got one Song!"

Hailing midfielder Alex Song

"We love you Freddie. Because you've got red hair. We love you Freddie. Because you're everywhere. We love you Freddie. You're Arsenal through and through."

To the tune of Can't Take My Eyes Off You

"Lasagne, woah-oh. Lasagne, woah-oh. We laughed ourselves to bits. When Tottenham got the sh*ts!"

After Spurs missed out on the top four when six players had food poisoning

"Vieira, woah-oh. Vieira, woah-oh. He came from Senegal. To play for Arsenal!"

To the tune of Volare

"Shall we score a goal for you?"

Gunners fans' response to Celtic's "Shall we sing a song for you?"

"You won the league in black and white. You won the league in black and white. You won the league in the 60s. You won the league in black and white."

Laughing at Spurs, to the tune of Saints Go Marching In

"He's five foot four. He's five foot four. We've got Arshavin. F*ck Adebayor!"

Arsenal fans hail their new, ahem, 5ft 8in Russian striker

"Gareth Bale peels bananas in Madrid. Bananas in Madrid. Bananas in Madrid. Gareth Bale peels bananas in Madrid..."

To the tune of Yellow Submarine

"We like Eboue-boue. We like Eboue-boue. We like Eboue-boue. We like E... boue!"

Saluting Emmanuel Eboue to the tune of Reel 2 Real's song I Like To Move It

"Sagna, Sagna. Bacary Sagna. He's got dodgy hair, but we don't care. Bacary Sagna!"

The defender gets his own song

"Na-na, na-na, na-na, na-na-na-na now. Samir Na-se-ri. Na-se-ri. Samir Na-se-ri!"

To the tune of KC and the Sunshine Band

"You're just a fat Robbie Savage!"

Singing to Liverpool striker Andriy Voronin

"You're not ringing anymore!"

Aimed at Mr Portsmouth and his bell after Arsenal's third and fourth goals

"He came to us when Henry went, Eddie, Eddie. He scored more goals than Darren Bent, Eddie, Eddie. He broke his leg, but he'll be back. And Darren Bent will still be cack. Eduardo Silva. Arsenal's number nine!"

Recognising the Gunners striker

"Di-mi-tar, Di-mi-tar. His mum washes cars. On the north cir-cu-lar."

The fans to Spurs' Bulgarian star

"He's bald. He's sh*t. He plays when no-one's fit. Pascal Cygan, Pascal Cygan!"

The fans love him really

Printed in Great Britain
by Amazon